Customer Lessons For Product Managers

Techniques For Product Managers To Better Understand What Their Customers Really Want

"Practical, proven examples of how to get the customer insights that are necessary in order to have a successful product"

Dr. Jim Anderson

Published by:
Blue Elephant Consulting
Tampa, Florida

Copyright © 2013 by Dr. Jim Anderson

All rights reserved. No part of this book may be reproduced of transmitted in any form or by any means, electronic or mechanical, including photocopying, recording or by any information storage and retrieval system without written permission of the publisher, except for inclusion of brief quotations in a review.

Printed in the United States of America

Library of Congress Control Number: 2013956586

ISBN-13: 978-1494321741
ISBN-10: 1494321742

Warning – Disclaimer

The purpose of this book is to educate and entertain. This book does not promise or guarantee that anyone following the ideas, tips, suggestions, techniques or strategies will be successful. The author, publisher and distributor(s) shall have neither liability nor responsibility to anyone with respect to any loss or damage caused, or alleged to be caused, directly or indirectly by the information contained in this book.

Recient Books By The Author

Product Management

- How To Have A Successful Product Manager Career: The Things That You Need To Be Doing TODAY In Order To Have A Successful Product Manager Career

- Product Manager Product Success: How to keep your product on track and make it become a success

- Communication Skills For Product Managers: The Communication Skills That Product Managers Need To Know How To Use In Order To Have A Successful Product

Public Speaking

- Secrets To Planning The Perfect Speech

- Secrets To Organizing The Perfect Speech: How to organize the best speech of your life!

- Secrets To Creating The Perfect Speech: How to create a speech that will make your message be remembered forever!

CIO Skills

- CIO Business Skills: How CIOs can work effectively with the rest of the company!

- Managing Your CIO Career: Steps That CIOs Have To Take In Order To Have A Long And Successful Career

- CIO Communication Skills Secrets: Tips And Techniques For CIOs To Use In Order To Become Better Communicators

IT Manager

- IT Manager Budgeting Skills

- IT Manager Career Secrets: Tips And Techniques That IT Managers Can Use In Order To Have A Successful Career

- Secrets Of Effective Leadership For IT Managers : Tips And Techniques That IT Managers Can Use In Order To Develop Leadership Skills

Negotiating

- Preparing For Your Next Negotiation: What You Need To Do BEFORE A Negotiation Starts In Order To Get The Best Possible Deal

- How To Open Your Next Negotiation: How To Start A Negotiation In Order To Get The Best Possible Outcome

- Learn How To Argue In Your Next Negotiation: How To Develop The Skill Of Effective Arguing In A Negotiation In Order To Get The Best Possible Outcome

Note: See a complete list of books by Dr. Jim Anderson at the back of this book.

Acknowledgements

Any book like this one is the result of years of real-world work experience. In my over 25 years of working for 7 different firms, I have met countless fantastic people and I've been mentored by some truly exceptional ones. Although I've probably forgotten some of the people who made me the person that I am today, here is my attempt to finally give them the recognition that they so truly deserve:

- Thomas P. Anderson
- Art Puett
- Bobbi Marshall
- Bob Boggs

Dr. Jim Anderson

This book is dedicated to my wife Lori. None of this would have been possible without her love and support.

Thanks for the best 21 years of my life (so far)...!

Table Of Contents

WHAT IS YOUR CUSTOMER TRYING TO TELL YOU? 8

ABOUT THE AUTHOR 10

CHAPTER 1: PRODUCT DISASTERS 15

CHAPTER 2: GOOD GUESSING GETS GREAT GRADES 18

CHAPTER 3: LET'S GO VISIT THE CUSTOMER, PRODUCT MANAGER… 21

CHAPTER 4: PRODUCT MANAGER ARE YOU A "DATA DUMMY" OR A "KNOWLEDGE MASTER"? 24

CHAPTER 5: ARE ANGRY CUSTOMERS A PRODUCT MANAGER'S BEST FRIEND? 28

CHAPTER 6: HOW TO SURVIVE THE PRODUCT MANAGER BERMUDA TRIANGLE 31

CHAPTER 7: WHY CHATTY PRODUCT MANAGERS DO WELL ON THE WEB 2.0 35

CHAPTER 8: CUSTOMER LED NEW PRODUCT DESIGN: NOTES FROM THE FIELD 38

CHAPTER 9: YOUR CUSTOMERS ARE IDIOTS & YOU NEED TO TELL THEM WHAT TO DO 42

CHAPTER 10: PRODUCT MANAGER WOULD YOU SLEEP WITH YOUR CUSTOMER IF THEY OFFERED YOU $1M ORDER? 47

CHAPTER 11: TOO MUCH CHOICE IS BAD: CUSTOMERS DON'T WANT TO DO YOUR JOB FOR YOU 51

CHAPTER 12: HOW TO MARKET YOUR PRODUCT TO YOUR CUSTOMERS IN THE NEW YEAR 55

What Is Your Customer Trying To Tell You?

In the end, it all comes down to what your customer wants to tell you about your product. However, how many of us have been taught how to listen to our customers?

If only it was as easy as having our potential customers pick up the phone to give us a call and tell us what they'd like our products to do for them. That never seems to happen so product managers have to take a different approach.

The good news is that information on what our customers want our products to do is out there — we just need to know how to find it. Visiting the customer is a great way to get important product information if you know how to ask the right questions. Additionally, we all collect tons of information on our customers and our products, but knowing what to do with it is another story.

You wouldn't think that an angry customer would be able to help a product manager improve their product, but you'd be wrong. Angry customers will tell you in very clear terms what your product is NOT doing for them.

Your ultimate goal as a product manager has to be to involve your customer in the product creation process. Since your customer is the one who best knows and understands what their needs are, the more that they can contribute to the design of the product, the better your chances of selling it them are.

Finally, depending on how new or innovative your product is, your customers may not understand what it does or even that they have the problem that it solves. When you find yourself in this situation, you've got the job of educating your customer about not only their problems but also the solution that your product can provide them with.

This book contains the answers that you need in order to better understand what your customers are trying to tell you. It's a matter of understanding how to listen to them and then how to understand what they have been trying to tell you. After you've read the book, you're going to be a product manager who understands what your customers are trying to tell you better than anyone else!

For more information on what it takes to be a great product manager, check out my blog, The Accidental Product Manager, at:

www.TheAccidentalPM.com

Good luck!

- Dr. Jim Anderson

About The Author

I must confess that I never set out to be a product manager. When I went to school, I studied Computer Science and thought that I'd get a nice job programming and that would be that. Well, at least part of that plan worked out!

My first job was working for Boeing on their F/A-18 fighter jet program. I spent my days programming fighter jet software in assembly language and I loved it. The U.S. government decided to save some money and went looking for other countries to sell this plane to. This put me into an unfamiliar role: I started to meet with foreign military officials in order to explain what my product did.

Time moved on and so did I. I found myself working for Siemens, the big German telecommunications company. They were making phone switches and selling them to the seven U.S. phone companies. The problem was that the switches were too complicated. Customers couldn't tell the difference between one complicated phone switch from another complicated phone switch.

The Siemens sales folks were in a bind. They didn't know enough about how the switches worked to tell their customers why they should buy them. Siemens reached out into their engineering unit looking for anyone who could help the sales teams out. I put my hand up and overnight I became a product manager.

Since then I've spent over 20 years working as a product manager for both big companies and startups. This has given me an opportunity to do everything that a product manager does many, many times. I know what works as well as what doesn't work.

I now live in Tampa Florida where I spend my time managing my consulting business, Blue Elephant Consulting, teaching college courses at the University of South Florida, and traveling to work with companies like yours to share the knowledge that I have about how product managers can make their product be a success.

I'm always available to answer questions and I can be reached at:

Dr. Jim Anderson
Blue Elephant Consulting
Email: jim@BlueElephantConsulting.com
Facebook: http://goo.gl/1TVoK
Web: **www.BlueElephantConsulting.com**

"Unforgettable communication skills that will set your ideas free..."

Create Products Your Customers Want At A Price That They Are Willing To Pay!

Dr. Jim Anderson is available to provide training and coaching on the two topics that are the most important to product managers everywhere: how do I create the products that my customers want and what should I price them at?

Dr. Anderson believes that in order to both learn and remember what he says, product managers need to laugh. Each one of his speeches is full of fun and humor so that what he says "sticks" with everyone.

Dr. Anderson's Product Management Training Includes:

1. How can you segment your market?
2. What problems are your customers having right now?
3. Which of your customer's problems does your product solve?
4. How much of this problem does your product solve?
5. How much will it cost your customer if they don't fix this problem?

Dr. Jim Anderson presents over 100 speeches per year. To invite Dr. Anderson to speak at your event, contact him at:

Phone: 813-418-6970 or
Email: jim@BlueElephantConsulting.com

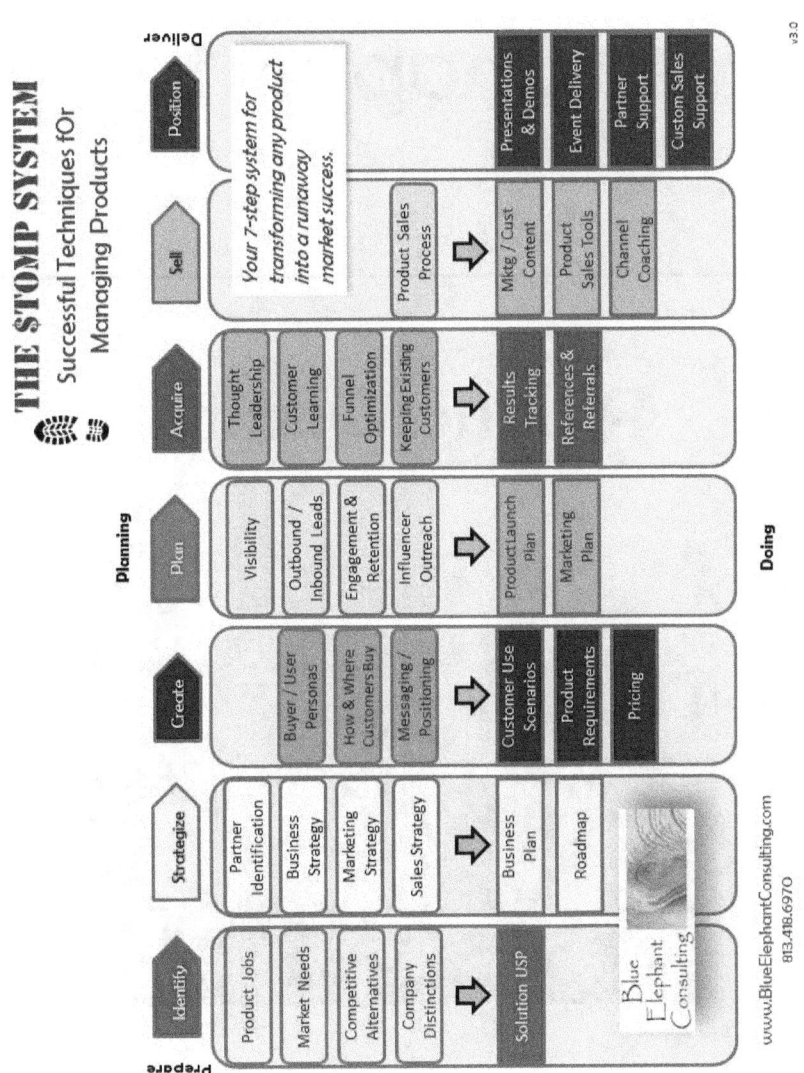

The **$TOMP** product management system has been created by **Blue Elephant Consulting** to help product managers know what to do and when to do it in order for a product to be successful.

Chapter 1

Product Disasters

Chapter 1: Product Disasters

We all have our own set of up close and personal product disaster stories. Just like when we're out driving and end up having to wait in traffic because there was an accident up ahead, we always hope that they won't have cleared it completely out of the way by the time that we get to the head of the line because we really want to see the horrible thing that happened. I believe that product disaster stories serve the same purpose: an opportunity to professionally rubberneck.

One of my stories (there are many) goes all the way back to the beginning of the '90s. I was working for a huge telecommunications equipment vendor who had started to believe the trade rags and had invested heavily in a new type of phone technology called ISDN.

Basically, this was a first try at moving from the old school analog signal over copper to a new all-digital signal. From the get go the deck was stacked against this product.

It was created by engineers for engineers. From a user point-of-view there was no really big compelling reason to switch. Oh, and if you did switch, then you had to get all new telephones and all new connectors put into the wall.

I've never see so many people work so hard to try to make a pig fly. It turns out that this was a solution in search of a problem. After spending way too much $$$ trying to push this product onto an unwilling public, ISDN slowly morphed into a form of DSL and is now finally being put to rest.

So what can be learned from this product wipe-out? First, you have to clearly identify what problem your product is going to solve (and why it's a big deal). ISDN didn't really solve a problem for the customer; it only solved problems for the phone company.

Next, you always have to be laser focused on just what the customer facing benefits of your product are. You always have to be broadcasting these benefits and then, this is key, listening to how customers respond. If they don't care, then you may have a dud product on your hands. ISDN had lots of extra bandwidth; however, in the early 90's nobody knew what to do with it.

Not every product will succeed. However, a good product manager keeps his/her eyes open and knows when to either change the product or walk away early in the game BEFORE it's too late.

Chapter 2

Good Guessing Gets Great Grades

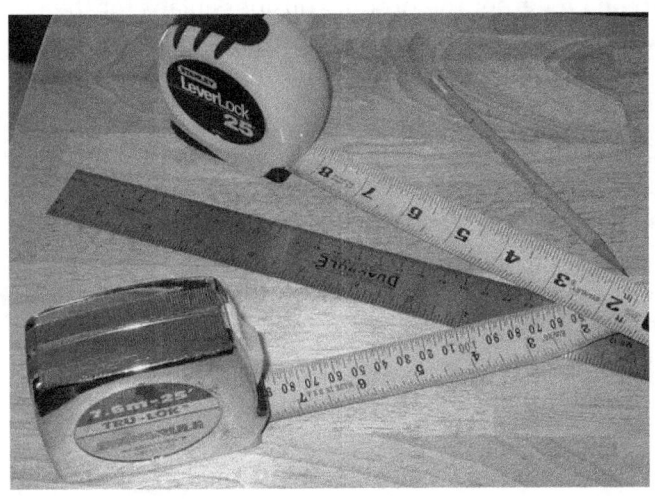

Chapter 2: Good Guessing Gets Great Grades

Who would have ever guessed that a big chunk of the art of product management would revolve around your ability to make good guesses? We like to call it estimating; however, at the end of the day it's really guessing.

The cruel fact of life is that he/she who does the best (most accurate) job of guessing wins the raise, promotion, undying gratitude of the big boss, etc.

So just how does one go about learning this black art of estimating? Well back when I was first starting out as a Product Manager I was working with a coworker named Dave.

I can clearly remember working until the wee hours of the night trying to pull together the product business plans for the next year. Dave was doing the same thing, but he seemed to be going home on time each evening.

I on the other hand was staying and building elaborate Excel models in an attempt to estimate budget, staffing, and time required to complete these business plans.

Dave and I both reported to the same manager who had been around the block countless times. When we turned in our product plans my boss took a look through Dave's, grunted, and put them down on his desk.

Next he looked through mine, didn't say anything for the longest time, and then finally looked at me and said:" ...*your estimates are all way too low*". Talk about being crushed!

On our way back to our desks, I turned to Dave and asked him how he did it. I mean I had put in the time, built the Excel models, and done everything with engineering precision. Yet, somehow I had missed the mark. What was his secret?

Dave then told me something that I have used to this very day. He told me that he really wasn't very good at estimating anything. However, he had taken the time to study WHY his estimates were wrong.

It turns out that his estimates were consistently about 1/2 of what they should have been. How did he solve this problem? Simply by doubling every estimate that he created. Poof – that allowed him to be on the mark every time! I took Dave's advice, doubled my estimates and took them back to my boss. This time around he grunted and accepted my business plans.

So what does this mean to you – should you just start doubling your estimates? NO! Instead, what you need to do is to pick one or more of your project estimates and collect metrics on how much that project actually ended up costing.

What you'll find is that you are probably off by the same amount each time (you will always be off!). This is the magic estimate number for you. Some of us estimate high, some low. but we all seem to do it constantly. My friend Dave has stayed with that firm and is now an Executive Director in the Marketing department. I've moved on; however, I still use his rule to create accurate estimates.

Chapter 3

Let's Go Visit The Customer, Product Manager...

Chapter 3: Let's Go Visit The Customer, Product Manager...

So much has been written about how important it is to get in front of your (potential) customer that I am almost hesitant to add to the pile. However, in reviewing what's out there, nobody really seems to have spent the time to lay out step-by-step what a product manager needs to do before and during a meeting with a customer. Well good news, today that changes!

In my world, a product manager would never be able to meet with a customer without having a sales rep along for the ride. This is actually quite ok. I consider the sales rep to be my wingman and look forward to meeting with customers.

Since we live in busy times I always expect the customer to be busy and for us to end up having less time with them than was planned. What this all leads to is that the key to a successful customer meeting is to prepare, prepare, prepare.

The best way to prepare to meet with a customer is to get your questions in order. By this I mean that you need to come up with roughly 10 different questions that if you can get the customer to answer during your time together then you'll have the opportunity to collect the real type of product information that you need to improve your product.

One of the reasons that you need to have a list of questions is that it will help you to shut up. Yes, you heard me right – the reason that a product manager visits a customer is to learn more about the customer's needs.

The more talking that you do, the less opportunity the customer will have to tell you what they want. Having good questions means that you can be actively listening to see if the customer is answering one of your questions instead of talking too much.

The world of sales has been doing this for a long time and they are actually quite good at it. One trick that they use is to come up with two different ways to ask each question. This allows them to re-ask the question if the customer really does not provide an answer the first time around.

Finally, you need to understand that you are not the only product manager in the world. There are a lot of them out there and they are also probably trying to get in to see your customer. If you were able to get an appointment, then they will probably be able to do the same. This means that you need to come up with a way to make your time together more memorable than anyone else's.

The best way that I've found to do this is to provide the customer with information that they can't get anywhere else. This can include late-breaking info about their competition or their customers that you pulled out of today's paper or off of the web. Alternatively, it could be some obscure feature of your product that would appeal to them or maybe even an update on your release schedule. Just make sure that it is important information to them.

Chapter 4

Product Manager Are You A "Data Dummy" Or A "Knowledge Master"?

Chapter 4: Product Manager Are You A "Data Dummy" Or A "Knowledge Master"?

Data, data, who's got the data? Thanks to our luck of being product managers in the 21st Century we are privileged to have access to quantities of data about our product and our customers that product managers of old could only dream about. However, is this really a good thing?

Dr. Peter Fader is a professor of marketing at the University of Pennsylvania's Wharton School. He spends his days studying how to use behavioral data to forecast product sales and manage customer relationships. What really made him famous was way back in 2000 when he testified at the Napster trial and said that Napster had actually boosted music sales!

Fader really knows his stuff and he's got some stern words for us product managers. When it comes to collecting data on our products and our customers, we've been doing a pretty good job. However, Fader says that how we've been using this data is not so good. He says that we've been attempting to make conclusions and future predictions that just don't hold up. Oh, oh. Looks like it's time for us to go back to school...

Fader says that what we are doing wrong is that we've just been doing simple data mining of our data. He says that what we need to be doing is to combine data mining with probability models. Can you say "math"?

Data mining is a great way to classify data. Specifically, if you are trying to figure out WHY one group of people is different from another group, then data mining tools and techniques are the way to go. However, data mining is not very good at saying WHEN things will happen.

That being said, data mining can be used to answer certain time-sensitive questions like what customers will order a given product during the holiday season. Where it will fall down is when you want to make a forecast about what particular customers might do in the future – not just what product they are likely to buy next.

What product managers have been missing is that our customers are creatures with random behavior. No matter how much data you collect about them or your product, you'll never collect enough information to accurately answer these sorts of questions.

At the end of the day, Fader reminds us that there's only so much that we can ever hope to nail down just by capturing more data.

What Fader suggests that product managers start to do is to use probability models along with data mining. What he's getting at is that for all of our talk about one-to-one marketing, we've really been missing the ball. Fader says because people are random, we can't really say what any one customer is going to do. However, we can say what a group of customers will do (just not what any specific customer will do).

Fader says that by using probability models, product managers can answer three important questions about their products: **timing** – how long will it be until something happens, **counting** – how much of something (arrivals, purchases, etc.) will we see over some period of time, and **choice** – if we give our customers an opportunity to do something, how many of them will actually do it?

If you take these three questions, you can combine them in a number of interesting ways in order to get answers to more complex questions. For example, how long someone spends on your web site during a month is really two timing counts put together: number of visits and duration of each visit.

So, to wrap this discussion up, what Fader is suggesting that we do is to start with probability models to create forecasts for how long a customer will stay with our company or how many times they will buy from us this year. Once you have this basic behavior captured, then use data mining to get an understanding of why groups of customers who have different behavioral tendencies are so different from each other.

Chapter 5

Are Angry Customers A Product Manager's Best Friend?

Chapter 5: Are Angry Customers A Product Manager's Best Friend?

In the world of a product manager, we spend our time worrying about defining, creating, and selling a product. All too often we view our job as being done once a customer has purchased our product – the next time we deal with them will be to get new requirements or to have them buy our next offering. However, all too often we overlook one of the most powerful forces in the universe – the angry customer.

I don't know about you, but in most of my product manager positions the job of dealing directly with customers who have already purchased my product was done by the customer service team. I'm no longer sure that my not being involved in this was the best idea.

Dr. Stefan Michel, Dr. David Bowen and Dr. Robert Johnston are European researchers who spend their time studying how customer service is done and they've made several interesting discoveries.

First off, the good Dr.'s have discovered that providing good customer service after the sale turns out to be just as, if not more, important than providing good customer service BEFORE the sale.

It turns out that your customer's perception of your company and your product are never fixed – they are constantly judging you based on the level of service that you are providing them with. This leads to two interesting points.

The first is that your customers are going to be judging you on how you handle any problems that they have with your product. This also means that they are watching you closely to find out what you are going to do in order to make sure that similar problems don't happen in the future. Guess what – customers won't be forgiving you a second time...

In the world of customer service, they have a name for the process of fixing breakdowns in a product. They call it "**service recovery**". How well this is done is what will have a very big impact on your customer's level of satisfaction, the possibility of repeat business, and in the end, your product's profitability.

If customer service is so important, then why do we seem to do such a poor job of it? The main problem seems to be that most product managers assume that the customer service department will handle any customer's complaint completely. This is not enough.

What a product manager needs to be doing is finding a way to address the underlying problem that caused the customer's complaint in the first place. If you don't do this, then the problem is bound to happen over and over again. And that is very, very bad.

It turns out that if a customer has the same problem with your product again, then you've pretty much lost that customer for life. There is almost no way to get them back. That's no way to manage a product!

So what's a product manager to do? The answer is easy to say, but hard to do. A product manager needs to find a way to get the customer, customer service, and product management to work together in order to fix the root cause of each customer service complaint.

Sounds easy doesn't it? Well getting these three teams to work together is quite difficult. In a recent survey, only 8% of firms do this well. It looks like you need to be spending your time working to make this happen at your company in order to make your product successful.

Chapter 6

How To Survive The Product Manager Bermuda Triangle

Chapter 6: How To Survive The Product Manager Bermuda Triangle

I can remember being something like 9 or 10 years old when I first learned about the Bermuda Triangle. I'm not sure where I first got my facts, but I'm willing to bet good money that it was that classic TV show with Leonard Nimoy called "**In Search Of…**" I didn't sleep for something like a week after that.

The basic story behind the Bermuda Triangle is that it is a patch of ocean (one side bounded by Bermuda) in which a large number of planes and boats have mysteriously vanished and have never been seen again. We product managers have our own version of the Bermuda Triangle: it happens when complaints cause our customers to disappear without a trace.

Whether or not the Bermuda Triangle is real, when customer complaints are not handled correctly a product can be made to disappear.

Dr. Stefan Michel, Dr. David Bowen and Dr. Robert Johnston are European researchers who spend their time studying how customer service is done and they've discovered another triangle which can prevent your product from disappearing. This triangle consists of your customers, the product manager, and the customer service rep. They just might have solved this mystery once and for all…

It turns out that customers who have a complaint are most interested in fairness. They feel that your product has wronged them and they want to have things put right. But that's not all.

Not only do customers want things put right, but they also want how the product failure was allowed to occur in the first place to be explained to them and they want to know what you are going to do to make sure that it never happens again. Oh, and they want all of this information in a reasonable amount of time.

Here's the important part: there's something called the "**recovery paradox**" in which a customer can end up being more delighted by a skilled service recovery than they were with the product in the first place.

My last experience like this occurred when I purchased an iPod adapter for my car's stereo system from the electronics supply store Crutchfield. I was installing the adapter, ran into some problems of my own making, and ended up having to call them for help. They talked me though what I was doing, pointed out what I was doing wrong, and solved my problem in about 10 minutes. I now love these guys.

The product manager's role in dealing with customer complaints is to use the complaints to change the product so that the problem never happens again. The key to doing this successfully is to ensure that there is good information flow between the customer service team and the product managers.

There have been some great studies that show that the more complaints that come in, the less likely a product manager is to talk to the customer service team – who wants to hear more bad news about your product? That's just wrong.

The final side of this triangle is the customer service rep. It turns out that customer service reps get the most job satisfaction when they are able to solve customer problems. However, they often get little support from product managers to do this.

In order to provide these front-line employees with the support that they crave, a product manager needs to make sure that they are equipped with the information and the training that they need to effect a service recovery. Additionally, a feedback loop needs to be set up so that the product manager can communicate the product changes that are being put in place as a result of previous complaints.

In the end, no one person can resolve a customer complaint. It really does take a triangle of staff working together to make sure that an angry customer doesn't get lost forever.

Chapter 7

Why Chatty Product Managers Do Well On The Web 2.0

Chapter 7: Why Chatty Product Managers Do Well On The Web 2.0

Boy, oh boy do I have a story for you today. I've been working with one of my product management customers who has decided that they need to improve how they communicate with their customers. Having read all of the industry rags, they've decided that they need to set up a **social networking site** for their company / product. Sounds good so far doesn't it?

This is where the problem comes in: **they want to control the discussions**. Oops, looks like someone doesn't quite get the "social" side of social networking. Yes, having your customers talk about your product can be a very good thing. However, in exchange for this potential goodness, you've got to give up some control.

No matter whether you set up your own social networking site or if you just use existing ones such as Digg.com, Del.icio.us, FaceBook, or LinkedIn, as a product manager you've got your work cut out for you. Since you can't control the content on public social networks (and shouldn't on your own), **you need to be a participant**. Replying to their comments and posting your own suggestions will make you a part of their social network.

Don't make the mistake that some product managers have made and try to pass yourself off as a happy and **satisfied user** – it generally comes across as quite lame.

Listening to what your customers are saying about your product can provide **valuable information** on changes that you need to make to your pricing, features, etc. What you'd really like to be able to identify are bloggers or commenter's who are sources of power – others listen to them.

If you can find these people, it would be worth your time to cultivate a relationship with them. Offering them free copies of your next product with **no strings attached** can be a great way to get a (hopefully) positive review out there just as your next version launches. However, keep in mind that you can't control the review!

I ended up working with my customer to make them understand that the value of a social networking site for their customers that their customers trusted (no content edited by the firm), was so valuable that it was **worth the risk** of the occasional negative product comment. They went ahead and implemented it and have been thrilled with the results that they have seen so far.

Chapter 8

Customer Led New Product Design: Notes From The Field

Chapter 8: Customer Led New Product Design: Notes From The Field

This chapter is an invitation for you to come along with me as I work with one of my product management clients to help them get ready to **present their solutions** to a customer in the hope of getting them interested enough to start to move forward towards a sale.

You'll recognize a lot of what we're going to be doing, but there just might be a couple of **surprises** along the way.

Meet The Customer

My client has already met with their potential customer and presented three high-level solutions to them. The customer appeared to be interested in all three of the presented solutions and asked for a **follow-up meeting** in which more detail would be presented. This is where things currently stand.

I got brought in to help out because my client doesn't actually have any of the three product solutions that they presented – they are all **POSSIBLE** products. Even if you've never done this before, you may have done something similar in presenting features that were not quite "there" yet...!

The Plan

When I sat down with my client, we started the discussion with the one question that every product manager should ask before meeting with a customer: **what do we want to get out of this meeting**? The client has a pretty simple goal: they want to collect enough information to slim down the list of three possible solutions to just one and get the ok to make a proposal for that solution. How hard could that be?

The Preparation

All product managers will recognize this challenge – limited time before the meeting with the customer. Since the three possible solutions have already been presented to the customer, this was the best place to start. However, **there wasn't going to be enough time** to dive deeply into any single solution – we were going to have to cover all of them down one or two more levels.

Face time was the budget that we had to spend. The meeting with the customer was scheduled for two hours in the afternoon. Clearly, that would be too long to spend doing a product presentation. My client and I agreed that targeting an hour for the presentation and the remaining time for pre-discussion and post-presentation wrap-up. Now all we had to do was decide what we wanted to talk about.

Planning The Presentation

My client had planned on doing the traditional In-Focus projector darkened room presentation; however, I talked them out of it. When I had asked them how many people would be attending from the customer's side, they had said that they estimated about four. I told them that since it was going to be that small of a group, it would be a better idea to change the "feel" of the meeting from a presentation to more of a **working discussion**. They liked the idea.

Presentation Content

This all lead up to what was going to be in the presentation itself. I pointed out to my client that they couldn't be neutral about this – which of the three solutions would **THEY** like to implement. For a variety of technical and, of course, financial reasons there was one solution that was the clear winner for them.

Every solution has its advantages and disadvantages. I convinced my client to present the other two solutions first and then conclude by presenting the solution that they wanted their customer to select. This was a variation on the **Goldilocks** "too hot, too cold, just right" strategy.

Finally, as my client was creating the material that they would cover during the meeting, I had them include enough detail for each solution so that the customer would be able to **visualize** how the solution would look if they implemented it in their company. The specific details of how it would be built or interfaced to their existing systems were left out – "to be discussed later".

Final Thoughts

As product managers it's rare that we have an opportunity to be present at the birth of new product let alone one that is being directed by a customer. When these opportunities show up, we need to be able to **guide the discussion** with the customer so that their pain points are revealed and we are able to design a product that best meets their needs.

If you can find a way to do this successfully, then you will have found out how great product managers make their product(s) **fantastically successful**.

Chapter 9

Your Customers Are Idiots & You Need To Tell Them What To Do

Chapter 9: Your Customers Are Idiots & You Need To Tell Them What To Do

It's expensive to create, market, deliver, and support a product. Having customers who make your life more difficult and the whole process more expensive does not help matters.

Since we're bright, smart product managers it sure seems as though when we spot an opportunity to change something about our product that will benefit everyone we should just go ahead and do it and **not have to wait for our customers to ask us to make the change**, right? Well that's what the product managers over at T-Mobile thought before the lawsuit...

The Problem With Going Green

... is that whereas everyone agrees that it is a nice idea in concept, most of us are **too lazy** to actually do anything about it. This is the problem that T-Mobile's product managers were staring at a while ago when they started hunting around for ways to cut the costs associated with delivering their service.

That paper bill that shows up in your mail every month looked like a nice juicy target for getting rid of. I mean come on, it's the 21st Century after all and we're talking about a customer base that is at least progressive enough to have a cell phone.

Think about all of the costs involved: printing, folding, mailing, and dealing with returns. If you could get everyone to drop paper bills and go with electronic billing then **the savings could be huge**!

As most companies tend to do, T-Mobile at first tried taking a "green" approach. They told their customers that they'd plant a tree for every customer who agreed to drop their paper bill and go paperless. This really **didn't motivate** very many people to sign up. See – what did I tell you about us being more lazy than green?

T-Mobile's next step was to start to charge an extra $1.99 for those customers who wanted a detailed printout of their bill. The exception to this charge was existing customers who could choose to get it without having to pay extra. Once again, **this didn't really cause any major change in customer behavior.**

The Big Stick

Clearly **the message was not getting through** to T-Mobile's customers – stop asking for paper bills and agree to switch over to electronic bills. In August of 2009 T-Mobile finally got serious.

They started charging an extra $1.50 monthly fee for all customers who had not switched over to electronic billing and who were still receiving paper bills. This fee **was applied to all bills**, both short and long, and it also covered existing customers – nobody got to escape it.

What's interesting about this big stick approach is that **it worked!** Before the new fee was announced, T-Mobile had about 1,000 customers sign up for paperless billing every day. Once the new fee was announced, this number shot up to 33,000 per day.

It turns out that T-Mobile sends out **16.5 million invoices every month**. At this new accelerated rate they had the possibility that they could convert their entire customer base to paperless billing in as little as 15 months.

A Lawsuit Can Wreck The Best Plans

Of course there always has to be an unhappy customer somewhere, right? In this case an unhappy customer was so unhappy that they went to the effort to **file a lawsuit against T-Mobile**. The suit said that the new fee was a *"...material modification to the contract by T-Mobile."* For those of you not up on contract language, it turns out that it's a no-no to make changes to a contract after both sides have signed it.

The T-Mobil lawyers took a look at this lawsuit and realized that they had a problem on their hands – it was legit. T-Mobile then promptly **backed off** and announced that they were dropping the $1.50 fee. Dang!

What Went Wrong Here?

So there are a couple of **interesting things** that a savvy product manager can learn from this T-Mobile case study. Here they are:

- **The Big Stick Works:** to an extent. Having an extra 32,000 customers sign up for paperless billing every day, even if it was only for a while, will result in a fantastic cost savings for the company. However, clearly customers didn't like feeling that they didn't have a choice.

- **Always Check With Legal First:** Sure, nobody likes the folks who work in the legal department. However, when you are messing around with a big stick approach to anything, it's probably a good idea to touch base with them before you pull the trigger.

- **Carrots Work Better Than Sticks:** Sure a stick is easier to use, but carrots work better. In this case waiting until a contract was over, and then making the $1.50 fee part of the new contract would have been ok – as long as T-Mobile also offered a gift or upgrade at the same time for customers who opted to go paperless.

Final Thoughts

If the number of people signing up for paperless billing now returns to their previous levels, T-Mobile estimates that it's going to take just over **41 years** to move all of their customers to paperless billing.

Clearly the T-Mobile product managers had their hearts in the right place; it's just that it appears that their brains weren't there also. Using the big stick approach can work, but it generally only works in the short term. If you want to have a **long term positive relationship with your customers**, then you're going to have to take the time to find ways to motivate them to take the action that you want them to take.

Chapter 10

Product Manager Would You Sleep With Your Customer If They Offered You $1M Order?

Chapter 10: Product Manager Would You Sleep With Your Customer If They Offered You $1M Order?

Would you sleep with your customer if they offered you a million dollars to do it? That was the question that was asked in the blockbuster movie "Indecent Proposal" with Robert Redford, Demi Moore, and Woody Harrelson.

Sure Demi Moore wasn't a product manager, but the situation was similar to the one that we often find ourselves in when we are dealing with a **manipulative client**. What should you do – take the money and feel dirty in the morning or refuse it and watch your product sales hit rock bottom?

It's Really Not About Sex...

In the world of product management, (hopefully) we don't spend a lot of time talking about sexual favors in order to boost the sales of our products. However, there are a lot of customers who **will do almost anything to get their way**. Couple this with product managers who have the inability to say no to a customer and you've got a recipe for a disaster.

I think that we all know what an angry customer looks like, but what is a manipulative customer? A little psychology textbook research shows that this type of customer is attempting to **both manage and control another person (you!)** , or a situation, in order to make things turn out the way that they want them to.

Before you blame the customer for manipulating you into doing something that you'll regret tomorrow, hold on a minute. All too often we product managers not only **allow**, but in some cases even invite our customers to manipulate us.
How do we do this? Simple: we make **two mistakes**.

First we have a deep need to seek constant approval of both ourselves and our product from our customers. Second, our greatest fear is that the customer will tell us that they don't like either us or our product and we'll end up losing our product manager jobs. We can't bear the thought of that happening. Shape up product manager!

Learn How To Turn Down A Customer's Improper Advances

Manipulative customers aren't going to go away – they will always be out there. As a product manager you are going to have to learn **how to deal with them** in a way that doesn't leave you feeling cheap and easy.

The first thing that you need to realize is that every manipulative customer has their own special way of twisting you around their little finger. Once you understand **how they do it**, then you'll be in a better position to prevent them from doing it to you again.

A case in point is the customer who has the way of turning your words around and **using them against you**. The next time you find yourself presenting to them, take the time to write out what you are going to say – perhaps even going so far as to use flipcharts instead of slides. This way you'll control the conversation and take away his greatest weapon against you.

If you dread meeting with a customer because of the **bad experiences** that you've had with them in the past, then you will probably be putting off that meeting for as long as you can and caving into his demands when you finally do meet with him. However, this just shows that you are suffering from low assertiveness – show some spine!

To solve this problem, you need to tackle the next meeting with that customer head on. Get it set up as soon as possible – **don't delay!** Then, before you meet with the customer, picture a successful meeting in your mind. What would you say? What would the customer say? Having a picture of success in your head will allow you to keep steering the conversation towards that idea. You're not assured of being successful, but this will certainly boost your chances.

Final Thoughts

In the end, you are not going to be able to get your customers to change their manipulative ways. Instead, you are going to have to **change how you deal with them**.

In the product manager job description we are told that we need to be **empathetic with them** and listen to their issues; however, just because they have issues does not mean that you need to make changes to your product or your pricing just to suit them.

Every time you deal with a manipulative customer, you need to **keep a record** of what they tried to do and how you dealt with it. As you have more and more successes, this record will serve to remind you that your own judgment is more than good enough to deal with customers who just want to have it their own way.

Chapter 11

Too Much Choice Is Bad: Customers Don't Want To Do Your Job For You

Chapter 11: Too Much Choice Is Bad: Customers Don't Want To Do Your Job For You

Shopping for groceries is a pain. Being forced to do a grocery store's job for them is **a bigger pain**. The U.K. supermarket chain Asda (owned and operated by Wal-Mart) is #2 in their market and they want to be #1. Their product managers have come up with a truly horrible plan to get there.

A Bad Plan From The Start

Sure, product managers everywhere would like to find a way to get closer to our customers. The grocery store business is no exception – it's hyper-competitive. However, over at Asda **they've gone too far**.

The Adsa product managers believe that they can gain more **customer loyalty** if they give them more of a voice in how the stores are run. Wait a minute, I don't really WANT to have to tell Adsa how to run their stores – I just want to shop there and have everything just be right.

One of the things that the product managers are going to do is to give 18,000 of their existing customers access to products before they are launched in the stores. Umm, where I come from we call this a **focus group**.

Touting this as a new customer outreach program is stretching things just a bit. It's also not clear if the folks **will get these goods for free**, or if they'll just be able to buy them before other people can. How excited can one get over having the ability to buy a new type of cracker before everyone else?

Why is Asda doing this? One of the drivers is that their CEO has publicly stated that he feels that customer loyalty **cannot be bought with points or discount vouchers**. Once again, what? I don't know about you, but YES my loyalty to a grocery store can be bought when they offer me discounts based on the products that I actually do buy!

The Thinking Behind A Bad Product Plan

As is the Wal-Mart way, Asda positions itself in its markets as a **low cost provider**. They spend most of their time advertising their competitive prices. This has not been enough for them to overtake the #1 grocery chain in the U.K. Tesco.

The Asda product managers are hoping that by involving their customers in making decisions about how the company is run, they will be able to build as much loyalty as the other grocery store's discount programs do. One technique that will be used is to put in **web cams** so customers can see how the firm runs: one at a local dairy, another at a carrot-processing plant, and yet another at the company's head office. How incredibly boring will that be?

Just to take the foolishness one step further, Asda will be building what they are calling a **"transparent store"** where glass brick will replace brick walls and customers will be able to see back into parts of the store that are normally not visible. I'm not sure about you, but I don't think that I want to see how the meat is being cut into steaks or the fish is being de-scaled. Some things are better left to the imagination.

What All Of This Means For You

Don't make the same mistake with your product that Adsa is getting ready to make with theirs. I predict that this new plan of theirs is going to have a **very short shelf life**. It is fundamentally flawed.

Yes, I can understand how it started – at an **Adsa brainstorming session** someone suggested making the company more open and letting the customers dictate how the company was run. Where things went wrong is that they missed the fact that I don't want to have to tell my grocery store how to do things, instead I want them to understand what my needs are and then shape how they do things for me.

The same goes for your customers. They really **don't care** about your product development process or what your product support area looks like (get rid of the web cams!). They don't want to go to work for your company.

Instead, what they want are the product features that they need even before they know that they need them. They want support that is so good that you fix things before they know that they are broken. What they really want is for you to **do your job product manager**.

Chapter 12

How To Market Your Product To Your Customers In The New Year

Chapter 12: How To Market Your Product To Your Customers In The New Year

The end of the calendar year is always a busy time for product managers. Even as your sales teams are running around trying to close the year out on a high note you as a product manager need to start to set your sights on what you're going to do to get ready for next year. **Got a plan**?

Uncertainty Rules

No matter what happens with the global economy, things aren't going to get better overnight. This means that your customers are going to be living in a land of **uncertainty** next year also.

As a product manager the role that you can play next year is to be a **source of both security and calm consistency** for your existing and potential customers. You can do this by providing your sales teams with solution facts and industry information that they can share with your customers in order to answer their questions.

Even Less Time Is Available

At your customers, the key people who are required to make the decision to buy your product will have even **less time** to spend thinking about your product than ever. This means that you're really going to have to start doing your homework.

Your communication with your sales teams is going to have to become a **lot more frequent**. You are going to have to start equipping them with new and different things that they are going to be able to share with your potential customers.

Too Much Data, Not Enough Knowledge

Welcome to the 21st Century. Your customers will have access to an almost **unlimited amount of data**; however, it's going to be harder than ever for them to get the knowledge that they need.

This means that in your marketing for your product you are going to have to become **the source of knowledge** for the types of issues that your product solves. That means that 90% of what you send to your customers will have to be fact based knowledge that they can use – not product marketing material. The remaining 10% can be focused on your product.

Short Term Focus Syndrome

As though this wasn't already a problem, your potential customers are going to be **narrowing their focus** even more than they already have. You'll see this as they start to focus on how products that they buy can have a payback within 6 months instead of 12, 18, or even 24 months.

You are not going to be able to change this **mindset** - that will just have to happen over time. Make the urgencies that your customer is focused on your urgencies. Make sure that your marketing material tells them how your product can help them meet their short-term needs.

Baby, I Need You

Finally, as we move forward, your customer is going to end up **needing you even more than they ever have**. The only problem is that they don't know this yet.

Your customers are going to be looking for ways to improve their business, but they just don't know **what they don't know**.

They are going to be looking for help in getting a grasp on the "big picture" of the problems that they are facing. If you can help them do this, then they'll be willing to talk with you about how they can go about solving parts of that problem.

What All Of This Means For You

Even as most companies start to finalize their next year's budgets, you as a product manager need to get ready to finalize your plans for **how you are going to be successful next year**. It's going to be a difficult year once again for your customers and so you are going to have to change how you deal with them.

Realizing that they will never see the world the way that you do, you and your sales teams are going have to be **the ones who change** in order to see the world the way that they do. More uncertainty, less time, and a short-term focus will all contribute to driving your product actions.

You need to realize that you can become your customer's **trusted source of knowledge**. What you are going to have to keep in mind is that this can't be done overnight. Create a plan now and work the plan as we go into next year and you'll end up being more successful than you ever have been before.

It's from the forge of failure that the steel of success is formed.

Hard Work Does Not Guarantee Success, But Success Does Not Happen Without Hard Work.

- Dr. Jim Anderson

Create Products Your Customers Want At A Price That They Are Willing To Pay!

Dr. Jim Anderson is available to provide training and coaching on the two topics that are the most important to product managers everywhere: how do I create the products that my customers want and what should I price them at?

Dr. Anderson believes that in order to both learn and remember what he says, product managers need to laugh. Each one of his speeches is full of fun and humor so that what he says "sticks" with everyone.

Dr. Anderson's Product Management Training Includes:

1. How can you segment your market?
2. What problems are your customers having right now?
3. Which of your customer's problems does your product solve?
4. How much of this problem does your product solve?
5. How much will it cost your customer if they don't fix this problem?

Dr. Jim Anderson presents over 100 speeches per year. To invite Dr. Anderson to speak at your event, contact him at:

Phone: 813-418-6970 or
Email: jim@BlueElephantConsulting.com

Photo Credits:

Cover - By: Dell Inc.
http://www.flickr.com/photos/dellphotos/

Chapter 1 - By: Ross Hawkes
http://www.flickr.com/photos/lichfieldlive/

Chapter 2 - By: Pat Pilon
http://www.flickr.com/photos/pat00139/

Chapter 3 - By: Ministry of Foreign Affairs of the Republic of Poland
http://www.flickr.com/photos/polandmfa/

Chapter 4 - By: Images Money
http://www.flickr.com/photos/59937401@N07/

Chapter 5 - By: Gordon Ednie
http://www.flickr.com/photos/gordon2208/

Chapter 6 - By: istanbul mohammad
http://www.flickr.com/photos/mohammadistanbul/

Chapter 7 - By: Lloyd Dewolf
http://www.flickr.com/photos/foolswisdom/

Chapter 8 - By: AudioVisualGifts
http://www.flickr.com/photos/audiovisualgifts/

Chapter 9 - By: Matthew Stevens
http://www.flickr.com/photos/krazykritter/

Chapter 10 – By: lordcima
http://www.flickr.com/photos/cima/

Chapter 11 - By: derrickting
http://www.flickr.com/photos/derrickding/

Chapter 12 - By: Sean MacEntee
http://www.flickr.com/photos/smemon/

Other Books By The Author

Product Management

- How To Have A Successful Product Manager Career: The Things That You Need To Be Doing TODAY In Order To Have A Successful Product Manager Career

- Product Manager Product Success: How to keep your product on track and make it become a success

- Communication Skills For Product Managers: The Communication Skills That Product Managers Need To Know How To Use In Order To Have A Successful Product

- Customer Lessons For Product Managers: Techniques For Product Managers To Better Understand What Their Customers Really Want

Public Speaking

- Secrets To Planning The Perfect Speech

- Secrets To Organizing The Perfect Speech: How to organize the best speech of your life!

- Secrets To Creating The Perfect Speech: How to create a speech that will make your message be remembered forever!

- How To Rehearse In Order To Give The Perfect Speech: How to effectively rehearse your next speech to that your message be remembered forever!

CIO Skills

- CIO Business Skills: How CIOs can work effectively with the rest of the company!

- Managing Your CIO Career: Steps That CIOs Have To Take In Order To Have A Long And Successful Career

- CIO Communication Skills Secrets: Tips And Techniques For CIOs To Use In Order To Become Better Communicators

- How CIOs Can Make Innovation Happen: Tips And Techniques For CIOs To Use In Order To Make Innovation Happen In Their IT Department

IT Manager Skills

- IT Manager Budgeting Skills

- IT Manager Career Secrets: Tips And Techniques That IT Managers Can Use In Order To Have A Successful Career

- Secrets Of Effective Leadership For IT Managers : Tips And Techniques That IT Managers Can Use In Order To Develop Leadership Skills

Negotiating

- Preparing For Your Next Negotiation: What You Need To Do BEFORE A Negotiation Starts In Order To Get The Best Possible Deal

- How To Open Your Next Negotiation: How To Start A Negotiation In Order To Get The Best Possible Outcome

Miscellaneous

- Power Distribution Unit (PDU) Secrets: What Everyone Who Works In A Data Center Needs To Know!

- Making The Jump: How To Land Your Dream Job When You Get Out Of College!

Techniques For Product Managers To Better Understand What Their Customers Really Want

> This book has been written with one goal in mind – to show you how to find out what your customers really want from your product. We're going to show you how to listen to what your customers are really telling you.
>
> **Let's Make Your Product A Success!**

What You'll Find Inside:

- **LET'S GO VISIT THE CUSTOMER, PRODUCT MANAGER**
- **ARE ANGRY CUSTOMERS A PRODUCT MANAGER'S BEST FRIEND?**
- **CUSTOMER LED NEW PRODUCT DESIGN: NOTES FROM THE FIELD**
- **YOUR CUSTOMERS ARE IDIOTS & YOU NEED TO TELL THEM WHAT TO DO**

Dr. Jim Anderson brings his 4 college degrees coupled with over 25 years of real-world experience to this book. He's managed products at some of the world's largest firms as well as at start-ups. He's going to show you what you need to do in order to make your career a success!

www.ingramcontent.com/pod-product-compliance
Lightning Source LLC
Chambersburg PA
CBHW071810170526
45167CB00003B/1258